This edition published by Parragon Books Ltd in 2017

Parragon Books Ltd
Chartist House
15–17 Trim Street
Bath BA1 1HA, UK
www.parragon.com

Copyright © Parragon Books Ltd 2017

Illustrated by: Giuditta Gaviraghi
Reading consultant: Geraldine Taylor

All rights reserved. No part of this publication may be reproduced, stored in a retrieval system or transmitted, in any form or by any means, electronic, mechanical, photocopying, recording or otherwise, without the prior permission of the copyright holder.

ISBN 978-1-4748-6310-0

Printed in China

FIRST READERS

The Three Little Pigs

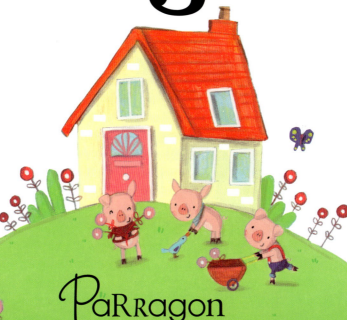

PaRRagon

Bath • New York • Cologne • Melbourne • Delhi
Hong Kong • Shenzhen • Singapore

Five steps for enjoyable reading

Traditional stories and fairy tales are a great way to begin reading practice. The stories and characters are familiar and lively. Follow the steps below to help your child become a confident and independent reader.

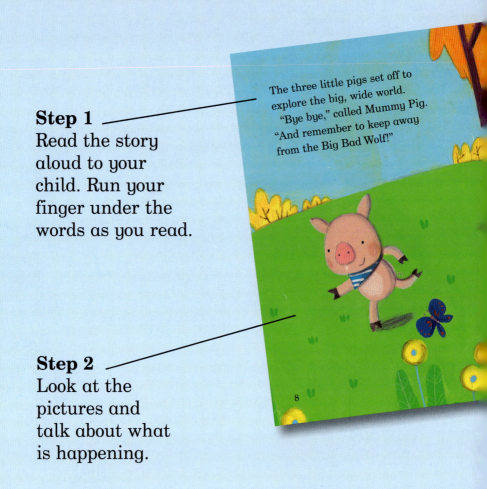

Step 1
Read the story aloud to your child. Run your finger under the words as you read.

Step 2
Look at the pictures and talk about what is happening.

Step 3
Read the simple text on the right-hand page together. When reading, some words come up again and again, such as **the**, **to** or **and**. Your child will quickly learn to recognize these high-frequency words by sight.

The three little pigs set off.

Step 4
When your child is ready, encourage them to read the simple lines on their own.

Step 5
Help your child to complete the puzzles at the back of the book.

The three little pigs set off to explore the big, wide world.
"Bye bye," called Mummy Pig. "And remember to keep away from the Big Bad Wolf!"

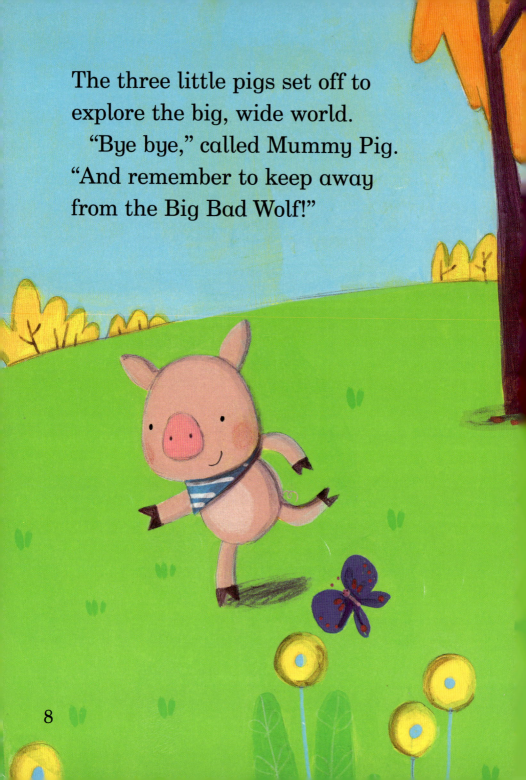

The three little pigs set off.

Soon, the first little pig met a man pulling a cart full of straw.

"Please may I buy your straw to build my house?" asked the first little pig. The man was happy to sell his straw. He was tired of pulling his heavy cart!

The first little pig made a house of straw.

But, that night, the Big Bad Wolf came to call.

"Little pig, let me in," he called.

"No way!" said the first little pig.

So the wolf huffed and puffed and blew the house down!

The first little pig ran away.

The second little pig met a man chopping trees in the woods.

"Please may I buy some sticks to build my house?" asked the second little pig. The man was happy to sell his sticks. He had been chopping them all day!

The second little pig made his house in no time.

But can you guess who came to call? The Big Bad Wolf.

"Little pig, let me in," he called.

"No way!" said the second little pig.

So the wolf huffed and puffed, and puffed again, and blew the house down.

The second little pig ran away as fast as he could.

The third little pig found some bricks.

"I'm going to build my house with bricks," said the third little pig to himself.

He carried the bricks to the top of a little hill. He laid the bricks. He hammered and sawed. He put on the roof and the windows and doors. His brick house took a long time to build.

The third little pig had a good, strong house.

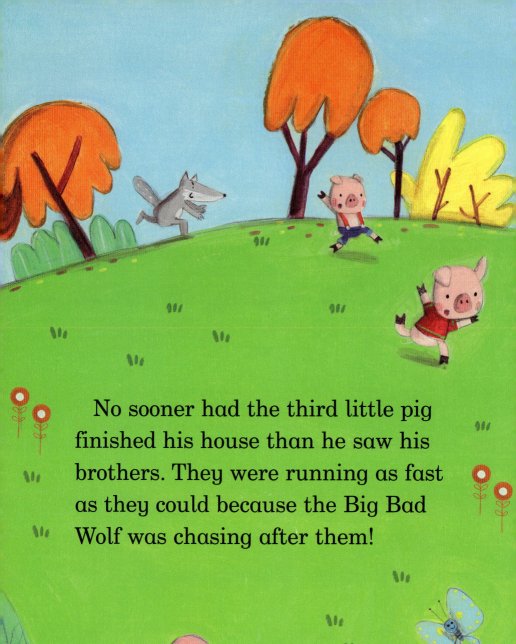

No sooner had the third little pig finished his house than he saw his brothers. They were running as fast as they could because the Big Bad Wolf was chasing after them!

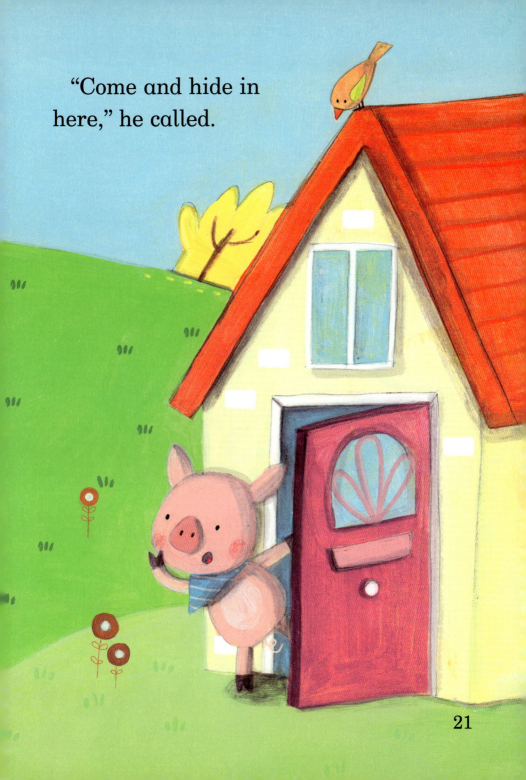

"Come and hide in here," he called.

The two little pigs came rushing inside and the third little pig slammed the door shut.

"Go away, you Big Bad Wolf," they shouted. But the Big Bad Wolf wouldn't go away.

"Let me in," he called.

"You can't come in," said the three little pigs.

So the Big Bad Wolf huffed and puffed. Nothing happened. He huffed and puffed again. Still nothing happened. The Big Bad Wolf blew so hard he made himself dizzy. The three little pigs were safe inside the brick house.

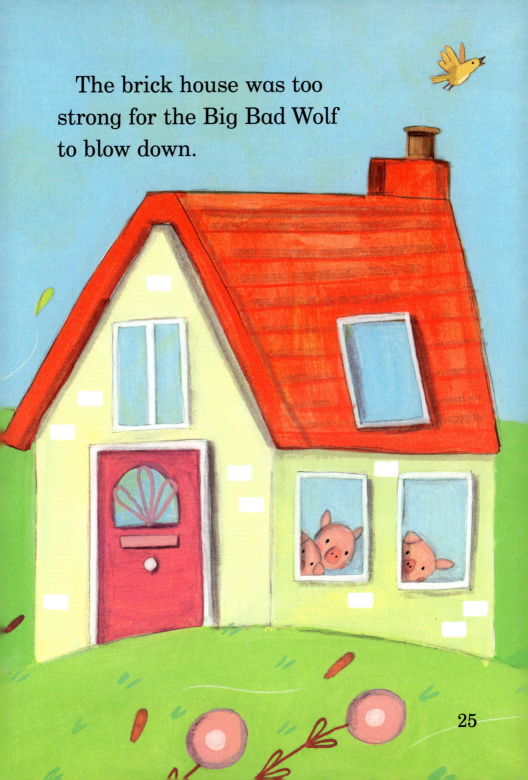

The brick house was too strong for the Big Bad Wolf to blow down.

"I'm coming to get you," growled the Big Bad Wolf. He started to climb down the chimney.

The three little pigs were cooking a big pot of hot soup on the fire. The wolf fell down and landed, plop, in the soup!

"Yow!" he shouted and ran out of the house as fast as he could!

And the three little pigs never saw the Big Bad Wolf again.

Puzzle time!

Which two words rhyme?

his bad big run pig

Which word does not match the picture?

house
straw
chimney

Which word matches the picture?

brick
stick
click

Who fell in the pot?

first little pig
Big Bad Wolf
third little pig

Which sentence is right?

You can come in.
You can't come in.

Answers
Which two words rhyme? **big and pig**
Which word does not match the picture? **chimney**
Which word matches the picture? **stick**
Who fell in the pot? **Big Bad Wolf**
Which sentence is right? **You can't come in.**